HOT TODDIES

Hot Toddies

Mulled Wine, Buttered Rum, Spiced Cider, and Other Soul-Warming Winter Drinks

Christopher B. O'Hara

Photographs by William A. Nash

Clarkson Potter/Publishers
New York

Published by Clarkson Potter/Publishers, New York, New York.
Member of the Crown Publishing Group, a division of Random House, Inc.
www.randomhouse.com

CLARKSON N. POTTER is a trademark, and POTTER and colophon are registered trademarks of
Random House, Inc.

Printed in the United States of America

Design by Jane Treuhaft

Library of Congress Cataloging-in-Publication Data
O'Hara, Christopher B.
Hot toddies / Christopher O'Hara—1st ed.
Includes index.
1. Beverages.   2. Christmas cookery.   I. Title.
TX815.0353   2002
641.8'7—dc21   2001057792

ISBN 0-609-61007-4

10   9   8   7

First Edition

ACKNOWLEDGMENTS

Unless you're Bukowski or Hemingway, most writers who have a penchant for quaffing cocktails don't get paid to write about it. Thanks to Chris Pavone, who conceptualized this book.

While Chris acquired the book, the person behind the editorial details is Adina Steiman. Adina wields a red pencil like a neurosurgeon's scalpel; she did a great deal to turn a collection of drink recipes into a small, beautiful book that I am very proud of.

My thanks to Jane Treuhaft for doing such a wonderful job designing the book, and to Marysarah Quinn, Trisha Howell, Alison Forner, and the rest of the team at Clarkson Potter as well.

Contents

Introduction

It's the most wonderful time of the year.

—Eddie Pola and George Wyle

Between dinner parties, family get-togethers, and errand-running, winter-time can be a cause for exhaustion rather than celebration. The frenetic pace and expense of modern life can negate feelings of "goodwill towards men" faster than a revolving mall door on December twenty-third. While this book doesn't presume to restore the cold months to their bygone glory, it does contain a distinctive treasure—a wealth of steamy, spicy, luscious holiday drinks that can give the innumerable dinners and parties of the season a festive flavor that's more Tiny Tim than Ebeneezer Scrooge.

Taking the time to make an old-fashioned punch, or making eggnog from scratch rather than purchasing it at the supermarket, can bring warmth and fun to a casual get-together or make a holiday party truly special. Great parties are remembered for a long time, and the secret to making them memorable is offering something wonderful to your guests; showing your friends that you care enough to go the extra yard makes your guests feel special. Best of all, most of these drinks are dead easy to make (a lot easier than roasting a turkey).

I hope you will use this guide to both classic and new holiday drinks to bring back a bit of the old-fashioned, homemade feeling of hospitality, and as an invitation to have lots of fun at your next wintertime party.

INGREDIENTS
AND TOOLS

THE PANTRY

Allspice Allspice is the household name for the berry of the West Indian myrtle tree. Also known as pimento (not to be confused with pimiento, the popular pepper found inside your martini's olive), allspice is an essential ingredient in the Tom & Jerry, wassail bowl, and Grandmother's punch, to name a few. Used sparingly, allspice imparts a subtle but unique flavor similar to a mixture of cinnamon, nutmeg, and cloves. Some of the recipes call for easily available ground allspice, but most call for the whole dried berry. You can find whole allspice in gourmet shops, specialty stores, and online at dozens of sites.

Brown Sugar Brown sugar is simply regular white sugar combined with molasses, which gives it a soft texture and richer taste. Dark brown sugar has more molasses than the light brown kind. Brown sugar is a key ingredient in many traditional holiday punches, including mulled wine and the wassail bowl. It's also the perfect sweetener for tea-based punches, and you can't make chocolate eggnog without it. Brown sugar blends perfectly with liquor, mildly sweetening with a taste reminiscent of a freshly baked cake—the ideal flavor association for a holiday drink. To soften not-quite-fresh brown sugar, place a chunk of it on a small dish along with an apple wedge or a slice of soft white bread, cover tightly with plastic wrap, and microwave for 30 seconds. Discard the apple or bread and stir the sugar.

Cardamom Unless you mix your own curry blends, make Arabic coffee, or bake a lot of bread, you will seldom have the opportunity to grab cardamom off the lazy Susan. And that's a shame, because cardamom is actually a wonderfully versatile spice, adding a unique, pungently sweet flavor to coffee (sprinkle a bit in the grinds before brewing), coffee cake, and apple pie. A member of the ginger family, cardamom is usually sold as small, cranberry-sized pods that contain about 20 seeds, which are more pungent than the pod itself. White cardamom pods are the type most often found in supermarkets, but the green (not the black) pods stocked in Indian groceries may be substituted if you have trouble finding the white pods. For maximum flavor, purchase cardamom whole rather than preground, as the essential oils in ground cardamom dissipate quickly, resulting in less flavor. To make your own freshly ground cardamom, pry open the pods and remove the seeds. Then crush the seeds using a rolling pin or a mortar and pestle. For a milder flavor, add whole seeds to warm punches such as glögg.

Chocolate Chocolate, in its many forms, is an essential part of the complete holiday and wintertime bar. Use unsweetened cocoa powder to create chocolate eggnogs and hot chocolate drinks; chocolate syrup for an irresistible mocha latte; and grated semisweet chocolate to garnish an ice-cold chocolate martini.

Cinnamon If there's a more traditional spice than cinnamon around the holidays, I don't know what it is. Be sure to stock both ground cinnamon and a good supply of whole sticks. You'll use ground cinnamon to flavor hot punches, eggnogs, and coffee drinks, while the sticks look great floating on top of a hot punch, and make an excellent stirrer for mulled wine or a hot chocolate drink. Even though cinnamon is one of the most common spices, many don't realize that it is actually tree bark—specifically, the bark of the tropical cinnamon tree, a small evergreen. Harvested when moist, the bark curls into the familiar cinnamon-stick shape when dry. Although cinnamon sticks look wonderful, don't discount their power—they can be almost as pungent as the ground spice. One benefit of using the sticks is that they don't add the dark color and somewhat gritty texture of ground cinnamon when you're flavoring a punch or hot drink.

Cloves Love them or hate them, cloves are another quintessential holiday spice. The small brown unopened flower buds of a tropical myrtle tree, cloves got their name from the French word for nail, referring to the small spike protruding from each bud. Use cloves to add rich, spicy depth to eggnogs, punches, and hot tea drinks. Insert cloves, spiky end first, into whole oranges or lemon wedges to create festive centerpieces and elegant garnishes.

Nutmeg Nutmeg is the brown seed of the *Myristica fragrans* evergreen tree, which also produces the spice mace (the seed's outer membrane). Historically used as an aphrodisiac and stomach-pain remedy, it's the principal spice in eggnog and many other holiday delights. You'll also use nutmeg to create special holiday coffees, teas, and punches. Add ground nutmeg to coffee prior to brewing to give it a tinge of holiday spice, use it to gently powder the froth of a mocha latte, or stir it into mulled wine.

Vanilla Next to nutmeg, few ingredients are as essential to preparing holiday cocktails as vanilla. Germany's traditional Grandmother's Punch (page 48) uses chopped whole vanilla beans; vanilla-bean ice cream is a key ingredient in Classic Eggnog (page 28); and vanilla extract is used in all the eggnogs and many of the hot coffee drinks in this book. Vanilla starts its life as the pods of the tropical *Vanilla planifo-*

lia orchid, which acquire their characteristic aroma only after curing. When the pods are steeped in alcohol, their delicate vanilla flavor is released, creating vanilla extract.

PERISHABLES

Butter Butter is made by churning cream, the fatty part of milk, until it reaches a semisolid state. Butter is sold salted, in which salt is added as a preservative; and "sweet," meaning that it has no salt. Sweet butter adds richness to just one holiday classic in this book: Hot Buttered Rum (page 40).

Eggs To make classic eggnogs from scratch, you'll need to break a few eggs. As unappetizing as it might sound, raw eggs are the key to making eggnog and its many variations. All the eggnog recipes require you to first separate the yolks from the whites. Usually, the yolks will be stirred with sugar, cocoa, and vanilla to form a batter—the basis of the classic eggnog. The whites are usually whipped until peaks begin to form, and then folded into fresh whipped cream to thicken the topping. You may opt for prepackaged eggnog mixes for fear that a bad egg will spoil the party—a legitimate concern, to be sure. A popular myth holds that in alcoholic eggnogs, the liquor will "cook" the eggs, offsetting any bacteria that may cause illness. The somewhat overcautious USDA disagrees, recommending against consuming raw eggs in any form whatsoever. If you are unwilling to gamble, buy the pasteurized, prepackaged mix sold in your local supermarket. If you are the sporting type, just make sure the eggs you purchase are kept in constant refrigeration until use, and purchase the freshest eggs possible.

Fresh Fruit No matter what cocktail you'll be serving, it's essential to have fresh fruit on your bar—at a minimum, lemons, limes, and oranges. Cut plenty of orange wheels, and lemon and lime wedges. Peach and apple slices are key for many of the punch recipes, as well as oranges and, of course, fresh strawberries. Try marinating fresh peach slices in your favorite liqueur for several days before adding them to your punch; your guests will get an unexpected burst of flavor.

CITRUS WEDGES Slice the fruit in half lengthwise, then quarters, then eighths. Cut a slit about a third of the way from the corner of each wedge so that it can sit easily on the rim of a glass.

CRANBERRIES Lush red cranberries are the perfect cold-weather fruit. Not only do they make for an excellent decoration around the home—strung in a

garland over the mantel or set into an evergreen wreath—they also make a delightful fresh garnish for punches. Cranberry juice is an essential ingredient for adding a tart-sweet tang to many holiday punches, and is mixed with Champagne in holiday cocktails such as the ever-popular poinsettia and the old favorite, holiday cheer. For a truly special punch, make your own cranberry juice instead of using the bottled variety by boiling fresh cranberries in a small amount of water until they pop, then pressing the cooked berries through a sieve, extracting the fresh juice. Purchase fresh cranberries during fall and winter at most supermarkets.

LEMON PEELS AND TWISTS There are three ways to make your basic lemon peel garnish. Use a citrus zester to make delicate wisps of lemon zest. Or, to make thin shavings of lemon peel, use a vegetable peeler or a small paring knife to cut razor-thin, $1/4$-inch slices of rind from the lemon, making sure not to cut into the white part of the peel. To make lemon peel twists, slice off the ends of a lemon and make a cut lengthwise around the lemon. Using a long-handled spoon, gently pry the skin off by slipping the spoon between the rind and the fruit. Discard the flesh or reserve for another use. Flatten the peel and cut it crosswise into thin strips. The strips should naturally curl into a "twist."

Heavy Cream Many of the hot drinks in this book call for a topping of fresh whipped cream. Although I am a loyal supporter of Reddi-wip, I encourage you to take the extra five minutes to prepare homemade whipped cream for your guests—you can definitely taste the difference. The key to making fresh whipped cream is getting your heavy cream nice and cold. This can be accomplished quickly by placing a small stainless steel mixing bowl of heavy cream into a larger steel bowl filled with ice. Since heavy cream contains about 40 percent milk fat, it is eager to form a solid, so all you have to do is help it along with a whisk. Merely add a small amount of powdered sugar to the cold cream, and make like Michael Jackson (beat it) using a whisk and arm strength—or better yet, use an electric mixer. After several minutes you will have delicious fresh whipped cream that you can use to top off hot chocolates and eggnogs.

Other Garnishes

Don't forget the Spanish olives (for martinis and Bloodys), cocktail onions (Gibsons), and maraschino cherries (Tom Collinses, Manhattans, and Shirley Temples).

THE BAR

Obviously, a good host should have a full bar at the ready—not only for alcoholic and nonalcoholic refreshments during cocktail hour, but also a variety of dinner-hour beverages (such as wine and beer), an after-dinner drink selection (which may include special coffees or teas), and perhaps liqueurs. Below is a guide to the items you should regularly stock that are essential to preparing many of the recipes. In general, the wines and liquors used in mixed drinks need not be of the highest caliber, but they always should be of reputable quality.

Brandy From the Dutch word *brandewijn*, meaning "burned wine," brandy can be any liquor distilled from wine or fruit juice—and there is a wide variety to choose from.

There are three types of brandy: grape brandy, made from wine, such as Cognac; pomace brandy, made from pomaceous (pulpy) fruits like apples and pears, such as applejack; and fruit brandy, made from stone fruits and berries such as cherries, blackberries, and currants.

What brandy should you use, then, in recipes that call for it? I always opt for Cognac, the brandy made in the Cognac region of France, which is distilled from excellent wine and aged in oak barrels. For mixing, or for hot toddies, regular (non-VSOP)

Courvoisier or Hennessy make excellent choices. For sipping, start with Rémy VSOP, and work your way up. Great brandy can also be had from Portugal, Spain, and even Chile. Greeks prefer Metaxa, a local brandy made from red grapes and sweetened with herbs. Fruit brandies such as Calvados are generally to be avoided in recipes that call for generic brandy, which refers to the less sweet, Cognac-type liquors. Save the fruit brandies for an after-dinner digestif.

You'll use brandy in most eggnog recipes, many punch recipes, and—of course—the hot toddy. So getting to know what brandy suits you is important. For punches and nogs, stick with the less expensive Cognacs, since the delicate flavors of the finer ones will be lost. But in the singular case of the hot toddy, where brandy is the principal ingredient, select a quality Cognac or fine Spanish brandy.

Gin

Before the fall of the czars brought Russian immigrants—and their vodka-drinking customs—to the rest of Europe and beyond, gin was America's favorite clear liquor. Made popular in England (London, specifically), gin is distilled from grains such as corn, rye, or barley. Pungent and tangy, gin gets its unique flavor from the distillation of a variety of herbs and berries (botanicals), including juniper berries, coriander, citrus peel, and black pepper.

Rum

This liquor is the distilled essence of the sugar cane plant, a member of the grass family that originated in New Guinea. Some rums are made with the freshly extracted sugar cane juice, and others are made from molasses, a byproduct of the sugar refining process. Rum gets its distinctive flavor from distillation (the process by which the fermented sugar cane is converted to alcohol) and aging (when the distilled liquor matures in oak barrels that once contained whiskey or bourbon). Any rum aged in an oak cask will eventually mature into "dark" rum as it takes on the flavors embedded in the oak. Rums range in color from clear to golden brown to dark black, depending on how and where they are aged. White (or clear) rums are not usually sipped straight, while the generally more complex darkest rums can be enjoyed as you would a fine Cognac. Rum, like scotch and bourbon, benefits from aging, which results in a smoother, less "alcoholic" liquor.

Rum is an essential ingredient in many of the punch recipes. Unlike some cocktails (planter's punch is one example) in which the rum is hidden by lots of sweet fruit flavors, most punches in this book seek to enhance, rather than cover up, the flavor of the rum—so don't skimp. Purchase a dark, aged (añejo) rum from Puerto Rico or Jamaica—and don't be afraid to experiment with lesser-known but equally good brands from the Dominican Republic, Cuba, and some Central American countries.

Tequila Made from the fermented and distilled nectar of the agave plant (a huge, artichoke-like member of the lily family), tequila is a fine substitute for vodka in many Bloody recipes. White or silver (blanco or plata) tequilas are the lightest; reposado ("rested" in Spanish) tequilas are darker, and aged at least six months; and añejo ("aged") tequilas are the richest and darkest.

Vodka For cocktails, you could probably stock your home bar exclusively with vodka and call it a day. Bloody Marys, vodka tonics, sea breezes, bay breezes, madras cocktails, martinis, and dozens of other highly popular drinks call for vodka. Originating in Poland, vodka was first distilled from potatoes, but now is made from other base ingredients too, including rye, wheat, and corn. Today's super-premium vodkas are superbly smooth, the result of a long distillation process that siphons off impurities. These boutique vodkas are great for sipping, but for mixed drinks, a moderately priced vodka is just right. To be safe, always keep a minimum of two liters of vodka on hand for a party, and keep another bottle behind the bar.

Whiskey Whiskeys are made from the fermented mash of grains such as rye, corn, barley, and wheat. There are literally thousands of different types, all varying widely in taste and strength, depending on what grain they are produced from, the length of the aging process, and in what type of container they are aged. The three principal types of whiskey to have on hand, in order of importance, are scotch, bourbon, and rye.

BOURBON Bourbon has been the preferred American whiskey for more than two hundred years. Made from a mash of grain that contains a minimum of 51 percent corn, bourbon is aged for at least two years in charred barrels. Kentucky is the true heart of bourbon country, although Tennessee whiskeys (the same as bourbon, really) are fiercely competitive.

IRISH WHISKEY More delicate and not as "peaty," the better Irish whiskeys can match the depth and complexity of fine scotches. The sprouted barley used to make Irish whiskey is dried in a kiln rather than over peat fires, and it's triple distilled for a lighter taste—perfect for Irish coffee.

RYE WHISKEY This whiskey is made according to a process similar to bourbon's, but it's made from a mash of grain with 51 percent rye. Nowadays, rye whiskey (also known popularly as Canadian whiskey—think Canadian Club) is more popular with the over-sixty set, and is found most often in drinks like Manhattans and old-fashioneds.

SCOTCH WHISKEY Scotch whiskey, which many connoisseurs claim is the result of the highest form of whiskey-making art, is available in two varieties: single-malt (or "malt") whiskey and blended whiskey. Single malts are made exclusively from malt barley that is distilled in old-fashioned pot stills. Sprouted barley is dried over peat fires and made into a malt, which is slowly distilled and aged for a minimum of three years, but often as many as eight years. While not as varied as wine, there are hundreds of regional Scottish malt whiskeys, distinguished by their own unique flavors. Blended scotches are usually less expensive and offer a smooth and consistent flavor.

Other Essentials

CRÈME DE CACAO This liqueur comes in handy for only one cocktail—in this case, the chocolate martini. Crème de cacao is a sweet liqueur imbued with the flavor of cocoa—it is, basically, alcoholic chocolate. There are two varieties: dark, which looks like liquid dark chocolate, and clear, which is perfect for chocolate martinis.

CRÈME DE CASSIS Used in the kir royale, crème de cassis is a sweet, dark-red liqueur made by infusing and macerating rum with black currants.

CRÈME DE MENTHE Yet another item that will gather dust on the bottom shelf of your bar is crème de menthe, the cloyingly sweet mint liqueur that comes both clear and in a bright green color. A noxious beverage on its own, crème de menthe is your secret weapon for creating several unique and flavorful hot drinks. A half-ounce added to strong coffee creates an eye-opening flavor and fresh aroma, and a bit more added to homemade hot chocolate is simply heaven on earth—a liquid peppermint patty with a kick. Opt for the clear version for mixing drinks.

CRÈME DE NOYEAUX Crème de noyeaux is a white-colored almond-flavored liqueur, used in the novelty holiday drink called the Candy Cane (page 75). Purchase it only if you decide to make this cocktail, although some like a shot of it in their coffee.

MANDARINE NAPOLÉON This Belgian liqueur made from Sicilian tangerines is one of the few sweet liqueurs that I've enjoyed on its own (Grand Marnier is another, and they are close cousins). If you're making the traditional Italian Riviera cocktail, you'll need at least a small bottle. If you can't find it, substitute Grand Marnier.

TRIPLE SEC Given the popularity of the margarita, triple sec is fairly common in the household bar. Although the literal translation of triple sec means "triple-dry," in the case of this orange-flavored liqueur it means "triple-distilled." Generic brands of triple sec aren't nearly as delicious as brand-name ones like Cointreau and Grand Marnier. Triple sec is key to making New Year's Eve punch, sangria, the poinsettia, and morning glory cocktails.

VERMOUTH Vermouth is a type of sweet fortified wine, infused with sugar and herbs. It can be drunk as an aperitif, but is most commonly used in tiny amounts for mixing martinis and Manhattans. There are two principal types: dry vermouth, which is white and contains 5 percent or less residual sugar; and sweet vermouth, which can be white or red, and contains approximately 15 percent residual sugar.

WINES

These days, "softer" drinks have become so popular that it's common to go to a party where only beer, wine, and soda are served. Wine also adds great flavor and depth to many of the winter-themed drinks that follow. Plan on two bottles of wine for every five guests. Double that if you are serving only beer and wine or if you are having a dinner party.

Champagne:
THE ULTIMATE HOLIDAY DRINK In more civilized times, serving champagne was a prerequisite for entertaining. Guests would be offered a glass of champagne immediately upon arriving, and glasses would be kept filled throughout dinner, ready for toasts. This formal custom has survived, but barely—usually just for weddings and other special events. Try to have at least some bubbly at all of your parties—even if it's just enough for a single toast.

Only sparkling wine that hails from the Champagne region of France and adheres to the strictly regulated *méthode champenoise* may be called Champagne. Champagne can be made from three grape varieties, Pinot Meunier, Pinot Noir, and Chardonnay, and is often a mixture of the three. Its sweetness ranges from extra brut (very dry) to doux (very sweet), depending on the amount of sugar added during the second fermentation (the one that produces the bubbles). The most popular variety and the type most suitable to the Champagne drink recipes that follow, is brut. It's also the style you're most likely to encounter in your local liquor store.

Depending on your taste and budget, you may opt for vintage Champagne—a wine produced in especially good years. Some phenomenal years for Champagne were 1979, 1982, 1985, 1988, 1989, 1990, and 1995.

Also keep in mind that even if the tried-and-true *méthode champenoise* process that Dom Pérignon perfected is used in creating the wine, only wines from Champagne may be called such. That being said, there are many great wines that sparkle besides those produced in Champagne—especially those from Italy and California. Choosing a less expensive sparkling wine from California is the way to go when mixing a large bowl of punch; the subtlety of fine Champagne would be lost in the fruity mix.

SERVING CHAMPAGNE Champagne should be served in the proper glass: a long-stemmed flute or tulip-shaped glass, which enhances the flow of bubbles and concentrates the aroma of the wine. Make sure your Champagne is cold, but not too cold: twenty minutes in an ice bucket should get the wine down to about 45 degrees, the temperature at which its flavor and nose are at their best. Open the Champagne quietly and carefully: gently ease the cork out of the bottle, using a cloth napkin to guard against spillage and a flying cork. The cork should gently hiss as it is released—no more than that. Popping the cork is not only dangerous, it wastes the precious bubbles that are the lifeblood of fine Champagne. Pour your Champagne properly by placing your thumb into the punt (indent) at the bottom of the bottle, spreading your fingers around its barrel. Gently pour about an inch into the glass, allowing the head to dissipate. Top off each glass to the two-thirds mark, which will prevent any wine from frothing over.

Port Port is a fortified wine from the remote vineyards in Portugal's Douro Valley. As with Champagne, there are other countries that produce port-like wines, but only a fortified wine from the Douro Valley can be properly referred to as port. Also like Champagne, port is one of the most heavily regulated wines in the world: all the grapes that go into its production must be classified and graded, and only the finest grapes in a single year are made into port.

Of the more than ninety different varieties of grapes grown in the Douro Valley, only five are considered good enough for port production, and the variety called Touriga Nacional is considered the best. Ports can be aged in the bottle or in the cask. Bottle-aged ports are better, since the wine can age for longer periods without losing its richness and

fruit. Cask-aged ports lose some of that rich, red color, becoming "tawny."

There are several classifications of port based on quality. Here are the least to most expensive: ruby (an inexpensive port, aged two to three years); tawny (aged several years longer, and sometimes mixed with white port to create the "tawny" lighter red appearance); aged tawny (a high-quality port that can be aged for forty years or more); vintage character (a premium ruby—port's version of Beaujolais Nouveau); and vintage (the rarest, comprising under 2 percent of all port production—the best of the best, with prices to match). Great vintage port years are few and far between: 1970, 1977, 1985, 1991, 1992, and 1994 are considered the best recent vintages.

Don't break the bank buying a vintage bottle to make glögg—just purchase a less expensive tawny or vintage character port and stick to familiar brands like Sandeman or Dow's.

Sherry Sherry is Spain's fortified wine, produced in a small area in the southwest corner of the country. The entire universe of sherry centers around three towns; Jerez de la Frontera, being the most widely recognized, is known for producing the richest, darkest sherries. In addition to regional distinctions, there are two basic types of sherry to choose from: fino and oloroso. Matured in barrels, fino sherries grow a coating of yeast known as *flor* on the surface, which reduces oxidation and results in a lighter wine. Tio Pepe is a popular and widely imported fino sherry. Oloroso doesn't develop *flor* because it is aged in the open air, and the oxidation that occurs results in a much richer, darker wine.

To fully enjoy sherry you need the proper glass. Connoisseurs prefer a tulip-shaped glass that narrows toward the rim, which funnels the sherry's rich bouquet directly to the nose.

MIXERS

Bitters I've probably mixed a few hundred thousand drinks, but used bitters just a few dozen times—mostly to make old-fashioneds. Nevertheless, even the casual home barkeeper must have at least a small bottle of bitters on hand, if only to give the appearance of a true mixologist. Developed in 1824 by Dr. Johann Siegert to combat stomach ailments and fever, his "aromatic bitters" quickly found world renown as a beverage additive, rather than a cure. Bitters are, as the name clearly indicates, bitter. Made from a mixture of more than forty herbs and spices (such as saffron and cardamom), bitters add a dry, bittersweet tang to sangria, Champagne cocktails, and punches. Bitters can be purchased at any liquor store; "angostura" is the type you'll most likely find. Since you use only a few drops at a time, buy the smallest bottle.

Cider

Apple cider is made from pressed apples, and can be of varying quality. You will usually find the best cider where (no surprise) you find the best apples: farmers' markets, farm stands, and reliable grocers. Sweet cider is just raw, unfiltered apple juice that, when fermented, becomes hard cider. The recipes in this book that call for apple cider (Spiced Cider, page 38; Wassail Bowl, page 46; Dale DeGroff's Harvest Moon Punch, page 52; Cranberry Tea Punch, page 64) refer to nonalcoholic (sweet) cider. If you want to create your own hard cider, just ignore the jug of cider in your refrigerator for about a month, and you'll have some.

Ginger Ale

In the early nineteenth century, pubs in England used to keep powdered ginger on the bar so patrons could sprinkle some in their drink—a custom that eventually brought us ginger ale. Some of the old-fashioned punch recipes call for a tiny pinch of ginger; others call for ginger ale to give a tart, sweet sparkle to fruit juices. Ginger ale can be substituted for Champagne in many of the champagne punch recipes when making beverages for children, teetotalers, and designated drivers—just add less sugar. I generally like to serve both punches side by side (and usually put out a small place card indicating which is spiked) so non-imbibers can feel part of the crowd without having to ask the host if the punch has liquor in it.

Grenadine

Basically pomegranate syrup, red grenadine adds a bit of sweetness—and lots of red color—to punches, fruit-based cocktails, and kid's drinks like the Shirley Temple. A splash of grenadine can also be used in a punch to adjust color or to smooth out excessive acidity. Rose's (of the ever-popular lime juice) makes a quality grenadine, which can be purchased at any liquor store and at many grocery stores.

Juices

A good bar always has some tomato juice in it, usually for the sole purpose of making Bloody Marys. The problem with stocking tomato juice for the home bar is that you invariably wind up with too much of it, and end up having to throw away a whole can in order to make a drink or two. The solution is to buy the eight-packs of small cans that you can find at many supermarkets and beverage distributors. Another option is to stock some resealable plastic bottles of Clamato juice, a blend of tomato, clam juice, and spices. Mix vodka, Clamato, and just a drop of Tabasco sauce to create the perfect Bloody Caesar.

You will probably have a few screwdriver or madras (vodka, cranberry juice, and orange juice) drinkers, or some kids and designated drivers around, so be sure to have plenty of orange juice on hand.

You should have at least a half-gallon of grapefruit, cranberry, and pineapple juices—or even as much as a gallon of cranberry and grapefruit juices—for making drinks such as bay and sea breezes or sparkling vodka drinks that take a splash of juice.

A small bottle of Rose's lime juice should suffice for the odd gimlet request. For cocktails that call for lemon juice, keep a few fresh lemons and a small hand juicer ready.

Lemonade
If you're making a punch that calls for lemonade, make it from scratch rather than using a prepared or frozen variety. There's nothing better than the tart, natural sweetness of fresh lemon juice to perk up a punch. And there is nothing easier than making fresh lemonade: combine 4 tablespoons of fresh lemon juice, 1 teaspoon of superfine sugar, and 1 cup of water (increase all ingredients proportion-

ally for larger quantities). Use fresh lemonade to adjust the acidity in any fruit-based punch.

Simple Syrup
An essential part of the professional mixologist's armory is simple syrup—a mixture of water and sugar that dissolves easily into cocktails, sweetening without the grittiness of sugar granules. Also known as sugar syrup or *sirop de gomme,* simple syrup is made by combining equal parts of sugar and water and simply boiling the mixture until clear. You'll need it to prepare Champagne cocktails and sangria, and it's handy, too, for a whiskey sour, Tom Collins, or margarita.

Sodas
For every ten guests, plan on stocking these mixers: four liters of cola, diet cola, lemon-lime soda, and club soda; two liters of ginger ale, seltzer, and tonic water.

TOOLS

Cocktail Shaker
James Bond's unorthodox preference for martinis—shaken, not stirred—created a resurgence for the drink in the 1960s that has lasted to this day. Part of the allure of the martini is the almost scientific attention to detail involved and, of course, the use of cool bar equipment like the cocktail shaker.

Back in the late nineteenth century, shakers were simple affairs—usually just two glasses of slightly different size whose mouths fit tightly together. During the twenties, the golden age of the cocktail, they became more elaborate, and strainers were added.

Stainless steel is the bartenders' material of choice since it chills beverages quickly. Be sure to have a long-handled spoon to go along with your shaker.

Gelatin Ring Mold

A gelatin mold is perfect for making ice rings. Ice rings—frozen circles made from the ingredients in the punch itself—are simple to prepare and keep the punch cold while adding a touch of glamour. Since your punch will likely spend a few hours sitting on a table, keeping it cold with ice cubes would only water the punch down—effectively killing it.

Choose your ice ring ingredients carefully to complement, but not overpower, your punch. For example, if the punch recipe calls for orange juice, make your ice ring into half orange juice and half water, adding some orange slices.

Grater

A multipurpose grater with small and large holes comes in handy for grating fresh nutmeg and shaving chocolate to garnish hot coffee drinks and cocktails like the chocolate eggnog and chocolate martini.

Punch Bowls

Nothing can spoil all the hard work of a special punch faster than not having the proper bowl or a large enough ladle. Even the largest salad bowls aren't really big enough to hold the amount of punch necessary to serve even a small crowd. If you don't happen to have a punch bowl or another vessel of such titanic proportions, visit a kitchen- or houseware store or check with your local caterers: they often sell or rent them for a reasonable price. Make sure to get some ladles while you're at it, preferably those big enough for the task at hand—dispensing cup-sized portions of liquid.

Whisk

For preparing a traditional eggnog, you'll need a good wire whisk to beat the egg yolk batter and to whip the egg whites for the topping.

Other Equipment

Last, but not least, don't forget the cocktail napkins, plastic stirrers, and toothpicks (for spearing garnishes). Make sure to have a half-pound of ice for each guest—it's surprising how quickly ice disappears at parties. And put out a large, ice-filled container: it's essential for keeping your wine and beer cold but not hidden away in the fridge. Ice the bottles down about a half-hour before your guests arrive, being sure not to overfill the container with ice at first (you'll need to continually add ice throughout the party).

2

NOGS, CIDERS, AND TODDIES

Classic Eggnog

PHOTOGRAPH ON PAGE 30

Eggnog is perhaps the most traditional holiday drink, and it has taken on many variations since its humble beginnings in the Britain of yore. Back then, it was known as "dry sack posset," a mixture of sherry, eggs, and milk. One theory on the etymology of the word eggnog *is that it comes from the British slang for strong ale:* nog. *Another theory is that the name stems from the word* noggin, *which often referred to a small wooden mug. Whatever the case, eggnog and its many variations have become a worldwide tradition. While the liquor may differ, with brandy in England, bourbon in America, and rum in Puerto Rico's coquito, the main ingredients are the same: a thick batter of eggs, milk, and sugar. Don't fall for the eggnog sold in supermarkets—it's a poor imitation of the original.*

SERVES 24

24 large eggs
2 cups sugar
1 liter brandy (or bourbon)
1 quart heavy cream
2 quarts whole milk
1 quart good vanilla ice cream, softened
Pinch of salt
Freshly ground nutmeg, for garnish

Separate the eggs into two bowls—one for the whites, the other for yolks.

Add the sugar to the yolks, and beat briskly with a wire whisk until thick and lemon-colored, about 3 minutes. Add the brandy and continue whipping as you add the heavy cream, milk, and softened ice cream. Set aside.

Add the pinch of salt to the egg whites and whip until they begin to form soft peaks (about 5 minutes). Be careful not to turn them into stiff, shiny meringue; the key is to get them just fluffy. Gently fold the whites into the batter until evenly combined. Chill the eggnog for about 45 minutes before serving, garnished with a pinch of nutmeg.

USING RAW EGGS

SOME HOSTS are reluctant to serve raw eggs. Although the food-safety folks at the USDA recommend against using "recipes in which the raw-egg ingredients are not cooked" especially when serving pregnant women, young children, or anyone with a weakened immune system, there is no way around using eggs if you're going to prepare a genuine eggnog.

The Food Safety and Inspection Service offers these guidelines:

◆ Select only clean, intact, and well-refrigerated Grade A or Grade AA eggs. Eggs left at room temperature promote bacterial growth more quickly, so be sure to store eggs in your refrigerator as soon as possible, and keep them refrigerated at 45°F. or lower.

Don't store eggs in the refrigerator door, since it's often the warmest part of the refrigerator.

◆ Use eggs within three to five weeks. Never store raw eggs out of the shell in the refrigerator. Also avoid having eggs outside of the refrigerator for more than two hours.

◆ As with poultry, be sure to wash countertops and utensils that come into contact with raw eggs immediately, as well as your hands.

If you follow these general guidelines, you should have a safe and salmonella-free holiday. But if you are really worried, there are many varieties of pasteurized imitation eggnog products on the market during the holiday season that you can serve, doctored up with a little nutmeg.

ABOVE: **Classic Eggnog** (*recipe page 28*). OPPOSITE: **Chocolate Eggnog** (*recipe page 32*).

Chocolate Eggnog

PHOTOGRAPH ON PAGE 31

It took me a long time to get used to drinking traditional eggnog during the holidays. I liked eggs, but couldn't stand the thought of drinking raw ones. Fortunately, my combined love of rum and Christmas eventually got me over it, but some people still have trouble. For those folks, there's chocolate eggnog. It seems that chocolate can overcome any fear of eggs, and by replacing the rum with more milk, you can even make an alcohol-free chocolate nog.

SERVES 15

For the Batter:
8 large eggs (see page 29)
1½ cups unsweetened cocoa powder
1 cup packed brown sugar
2 tablespoons vanilla extract
4 cups whole milk
8 ounces dark rum

For the Chocolate Whipped Cream:
4 ounces milk chocolate
3 cups heavy cream, well-chilled
Pinch of salt

For the Garnish:

8 ounces semisweet chocolate, grated

15 cinnamon sticks

MAKE THE BATTER:

Separate the eggs, depositing yolks and whites into two separate bowls. Place the whites, covered tightly, immediately into the refrigerator. Whisk the yolks with the cocoa powder, brown sugar, and vanilla until very smooth. Gently stir in the milk and rum. Cover the bowl tightly with plastic wrap and refrigerate for several hours until cold.

PREPARE THE CHOCOLATE WHIPPED CREAM:

Chop the chocolate into small chunks and heat it in a bowl placed over a saucepan of boiling water, stirring frequently until the chocolate melts. Cool briefly in the refrigerator, but do not allow the mixture to solidify. Meanwhile, whip the cream to soft peaks. Stir in the cooled, melted chocolate and blend thoroughly.

Remove the egg whites from the fridge and beat with a pinch of salt until soft peaks form. Fold the whites into the chilled egg yolk mixture and pour into mugs. Garnish each with a dollop of chocolate whipped cream, some grated semisweet chocolate, and a cinnamon stick stirrer.

Hot Toddy

Often, the best things in life are the simplest. The hot toddy—a mixture of boiling water, liquor, and a lemon twist—is one of them. Before there was Advil Cold & Sinus, the hot toddy was also world-renowned for its curative effects. The liquor eased aches and pains and distracted the sufferer from his woes; the hot water cleared congested sinuses; and the twist provided a refreshing dose of vitamin C (well, not really—but it's the thought that counts). I've always found that a few hot toddies can clear up a head cold faster than any over-the-counter remedy.

Hot toddies can be made with any sort of brown liquor—usually it's brandy, but you can also use scotch, bourbon, or rye whiskey. I personally prefer Irish whiskey. Add an ounce of cranberry juice to each glass to make a Cranberry Toddy.

SERVES 12

12 ounces brandy, scotch, bourbon, or whiskey
¼ cup sugar
12 lemon twists

Boil 3 quarts of water in a large pot. Place 1 ounce of liquor and 1 teaspoon of sugar into a mug and fill to the top with boiling water. Twist a lemon peel above the liquid and drop it in.

Tom & Jerry

The Tom & Jerry is eggnog's warm and creamy cousin, with the added kick of rum and spices. There is some disagreement as to the origin of the drink. Some claim that it was named after the two principal characters in Pierce Egan's popular 1821 book, Life in London, *Jerry Hawthorn and his sidekick Corinthian Tom. Other cocktail etymologists speculate that the concoction was named after notorious mixologist Jerry Thomas, a bartender at San Francisco's Occidental Hotel and the creator of the Martinez (the first martini, according to some). What's not disputed is that the Tom & Jerry offers a delicious alternative to traditional eggnog.*

SERVES 24

3 quarts whole milk

24 large eggs (see page 29)

2 cups sugar

Pinch of salt

½ tablespoon ground allspice

2 tablespoons ground cinnamon

½ tablespoon ground cloves

16 ounces brandy

16 ounces dark rum

Freshly ground nutmeg, for garnish

In a large saucepan, heat the milk over low heat until steaming; cover and keep warm. Separate the eggs into two large bowls, one for the yolks and another for the whites. Add the sugar to the yolks and beat with a wire whisk for about 3 minutes, or until the mixture is thick and lemon-colored.

Using a wire whisk or an electric hand mixer, beat the egg whites with the pinch of salt until they form soft peaks; set aside.

Add the spices, brandy, and rum to the yolk mixture. Stirring continuously, mix in the warm milk. Carefully fold the reserved whites into the batter. Pour into individual glasses and garnish each with a pinch of nutmeg.

Spiced Cider

A steaming mug of cider flavored with holiday spices takes the chill from your bones just as well as a roaring fire. Like most traditions, cider recipes evolve over the years, and each family seems to have their own secret recipe. My friend Tim Coleman simply melts a cup of Red Hots (the cinnamon candies) in a gallon of hot cider. Wonderful! Traditionalists usually use a variety of sweet spices, but spiced cider can be as simple as heating the cider and adding a cinnamon stick to each mug. It's up to you. Here's the O'Hara family's recipe, which is about as traditional (and tasty) as you can get.

SERVES 10

5 allspice berries

2 cinnamon sticks

4 whole cloves

¼ teaspoon salt

1 orange peel (whole peel)

1 lemon peel (whole peel)

2 quarts apple cider

¼ cup packed brown sugar

Ground nutmeg, to taste

10 cinnamon sticks, for garnish

Captain Morgan's Spiced Rum (optional)

Place the spices, salt, and fruit peels in the center of a 12-inch square of cheese-cloth. Gather up the corners and tie with butcher's twine to create a small packet. In a large pot over medium heat, heat the cider until steam begins to rise from the surface. Add the brown sugar and stir until melted. Add the spice packet to the pot and steep for 10 minutes, or until the cider is infused with spice. Serve in mugs with a sprinkling of nutmeg and a cinnamon stick stirrer. If you prefer spiked cider, add 3/4 ounce of spiced rum to each serving or use 1 cup of rum for the full recipe.

◀ Hot Buttered Rum ▶

Here's a concoction you won't see many vascular surgeons imbibing anytime soon; drinking butter is generally contraindicated. But the small amount of butter in the classic hot buttered rum won't hurt you. Basic hot buttered rum is made by simply adding rum to hot spiced cider, and serving it with a pat of butter on top. This recipe, which uses spiced vanilla ice cream as its base, makes for a smoother, creamier version.

SERVES 12

1 cup (2 sticks) unsalted butter
2¾ cups packed light brown sugar
1 quart vanilla ice cream, softened
1 teaspoon ground nutmeg
1 teaspoon ground cinnamon
1 teaspoon ground cardamom
1 teaspoon vanilla extract
12 ounces dark rum

In a large bowl, combine all the ingredients except the rum, mixing thoroughly with a rubber spatula. Place the mixture into a plastic container with a lid; seal and freeze.

To prepare the drinks, place 2 heaping tablespoons of the frozen batter in each mug, add 1 ounce of rum and ¾ cup of boiling water. Stir until the batter is completely melted. For a nonalcoholic version, simply omit the rum.

Coquito

If you're tired of traditional American holiday cocktail fare, why not treat yourself to something different and mix up a batch of coquitos, the eggnog of Puerto Rico. This Caribbean treat blends luscious coconut milk with rum to create an eggnog that will have you yearning to replace that Christmas turkey with a roast pig!

SERVES 8 TO 10

8 cups unsweetened coconut milk

¾ cup sugar

16 egg yolks (see page 29)

4 tablespoons vanilla extract

2 cups rum (preferably Captain Morgan's Spiced Rum)

Ground cinnamon, for garnish

In a large saucepan, warm the coconut milk until steaming, then stir in the sugar until it dissolves. In a large bowl, beat the egg yolks and vanilla until thick and smooth, about 3 minutes. Stir in the rum, and then slowly add the batter to the steaming coconut milk, stirring constantly. Be careful never to let the mixture boil, or it will curdle. When completely mixed, remove from the heat and let cool. Place in a sealed container in the refrigerator until cold. Serve with cinnamon sprinkled on top.

3

FESTIVE PUNCHES AND BOWLS

Mulled Wine

Mulled wine is a Scandinavian tradition that goes back centuries. Known as glögg in northern Europe, mulled wine is simply any dark wine (regular or fortified) mixed with spices and heated. Traditional mulling spices include cardamom, cloves, cinnamon, nutmeg, bay leaf, and allspice; most mulled-wine recipes also call for some fruit peel or fruit juice. The mixture is left with the spices to steep for a day or so, then served hot with sugar, often garnished with raisins, almonds, or dried fruit. Feel free to experiment with your favorite spices to find the mulled wine recipe that suits you best.

The recipe below is a fairly standard mulled wine, and the basis for several variations. I suggest using an inexpensive but still drinkable dry red wine—something fairly hearty that will stand up to the spices.

SERVES 10

Two 750 ml bottles full-bodied dry red wine
1 cup packed brown sugar
6 ounces orange juice, no pulp
2 teaspoons ground nutmeg
2 teaspoons ground cinnamon
1 teaspoon ground cloves
12 whole cloves
10 cardamom seeds

In a large saucepan, warm the wine over medium heat until steam begins to rise from the surface, about 7 minutes. Add the brown sugar, orange juice, and spices. Reduce to lowest possible flame and, stirring frequently, keep the mixture warm for 20 to 30 minutes, or until the sugar is completely melted and the spices fully integrated. Do not let the mixture boil—this will give the juice a "cooked" flavor. Strain and serve immediately.

Note: Refrigerate the mulled wine for 24 hours to really let the flavors come together. Before serving, warm it on the stove for about 10 minutes.

Wassail Bowl

Like eggnog, here's another drink that won't pass muster with anyone who is squeamish about germs. Back in Jolly Olde England, the Christmas Eve tradition was for carolers to head off with a large bowl of sherry-laced cider, which they passed from person to person. Since sips were often accompanied by kisses, the bowl was also known as the "loving cup."

Roughly translated from the Old English, "Wassail!" means "To your health!" Holding aloft the mighty wassail bowl, the leader of the carolers would cry, "Wassail!" and his no-doubt groggy compatriots would respond, "All hail!" They would go from house to house, caroling in exchange for a refill of cider. Most households welcomed the sherry-soaked revelers, whose visit was considered good luck.

SERVES 10 TO 15

2 quarts apple cider

½ cup packed brown sugar

6 cinnamon sticks

10 whole cloves

10 allspice berries

2 teaspoons ground nutmeg

1 vanilla bean, cut in half

1 cup freshly squeezed lemon juice (from about 5 large lemons)

Juice of 1 orange
1 ½ liters dry sherry

In a large pot, warm the cider over high heat until steam just begins to rise from the surface, about 7 minutes. Reduce the heat to medium, and add the sugar, the spices, and the vanilla bean. Simmer for 30 minutes. Using a long-handled fine-mesh strainer, remove the spices from the pot, then add the fruit juices and sherry. Find a large bowl, eleven friends, and don't forget your scarf.

Grandmother's Punch

Across the globe, there are very few people who take Christmas as seriously as the Germans do. Germans gave us the Christmas tree (Tannenbaum), the advent calendar, and Silent Night. Unfortunately, they also gave us . . . fruitcake. Perhaps in recognition of the dyspepsia often caused by ingesting rocklike fruitcake, Germans have also given us another holiday tradition: Glühwein, "glow wine"—their version of mulled wine. Grandmother's punch (Grössmutter's punsch) is an elaboration of traditional glow wine, which is nothing more than heated red wine with cinnamon, lemon, sugar, and cloves. Rich, smooth, and strong, this very special punch is traditionally served at midnight on Christmas Eve.

SERVES 12

1 cup packed brown sugar

25 whole cloves

25 allspice berries

1 cinnamon stick

2 vanilla beans, finely chopped

2/3 cup loose black tea

Two 750 ml bottles red wine

1/2 cup dark rum

12 cinnamon sticks, for garnish

In a large pot, combine the sugar, spices, and vanilla beans with 4 cups of water. Bring to a boil and cook over high heat, stirring frequently, about 5 minutes or until half the liquid has evaporated and the remainder is syrupy. Remove from the heat, stir in the tea, and allow to steep for 10 minutes. Strain the mixture through a fine-mesh sieve into another large pot and stir in the red wine and rum. Warm over medium heat until steaming, about 7 minutes. Serve warm, garnishing each glass with a cinnamon stick stirrer, or chilled, over ice.

SERVING HOT AND COLD PUNCHES

HOW CAN you chill that much punch? Simply make your punch in advance and refrigerate it in large containers until ready to serve. And be sure to chill the bowl with ice cubes, removing them only when you are about to pour the punch into the bowl. For hot punches, prevent the punch from cooling prematurely by warming your bowl with boiling water first.

For a sparkling punch, add the carbonated ingredients (Champagne, soda, etc.) last, to make sure the punch is properly bubbly. If you're preparing tea punches, avoid overbrewing, which can make the punch bitter.

For any punch, be sure to reserve some extra ingredients to adjust the flavor after you've mixed a batch. If a punch gets watery over the course of the evening, you can adjust the flavor by adding more liquor and fruit juice. A sparkling punch that loses its carbonation can be adjusted periodically with a splash of Champagne or club soda. Likewise, a punch can be sweetened by adding a dash of simple syrup (page 24) or more fruit juice.

FESTIVE PUNCHES AND BOWLS

◄ Glögg ►

Scandinavian aquavit, literally "water of life," has not made a tremendous impact on the rest of the world. Maybe it's because of the unusual caraway-seed taste. In the case of glögg, however, aquavit's unique flavor so perfectly complements the heated wine that it's like drinking Christmas itself. The best thing about making glögg the old-fashioned way is the theater involved in preparing it, so be sure to invite your guests into the kitchen to watch the pyrotechnics. You'll need a fine-mesh wire rack, which you should be able to find at any kitchenware store, to flame the glögg.

SERVES 12 TO 15

Two 750 ml bottles full-bodied dry red wine
20 cloves
20 cardamom seeds
½ teaspoon ground cinnamon
1 teaspoon ground nutmeg
8 ounces sugar cubes
One 750 ml bottle aquavit
½ cup raisins, for garnish
½ cup sliced almonds, for garnish

In a large pot, combine the wine, cloves, cardamom, cinnamon, and nutmeg, and heat over a medium flame until steam rises from the surface and the spices are infused, about 7 minutes. Strain, then transfer about half the mixture to a large bowl.

Place a fine-mesh wire rack over the pot, and arrange the sugar cubes on top. Pour the aquavit over the cubes, making sure to soak them well. Standing back, use a long kitchen match to carefully ignite the sugar cubes, then slowly ladle the reserved wine over them until they have dissolved.

Serve in mugs, garnished with raisins and sliced almonds.

Dale DeGroff's Harvest Moon Punch

Dale DeGroff is America's foremost mixologist and the man who nearly single-handedly ushered in the return of the classic cocktail. After twenty years tending bar at great establishments like the Hotel Bel Air and, most notably, the Rainbow Room, Dale now spends his time teaching mixology, writing, and consulting. He has kindly offered to share this amazing holiday punch, which has the perfect taste (and presentation!) for a great Halloween party. For a nonalcoholic version, just omit the bourbon.

SERVES 20

1 orange
1 gallon apple cider
6 cinnamon sticks
6 cloves
6 whole star anise
32 ounces bourbon
1 pumpkin, for serving
(optional)

FOR THE PUNCH:

Remove the zest (not the white pith) from an orange with a vegetable peeler. Combine the apple cider, cinnamon sticks, cloves, anise, and orange zest in a large stainless steel pot and let simmer (do not boil) for one hour. Strain and stir in the bourbon.

TO SERVE:

For a party, you can serve the punch in a hollowed-out pumpkin. Prepare the pumpkin by cutting a lid as you would for a jack-o-lantern. Clean the lid pieces by cutting away and discarding the pumpkin strands and seeds. Using a long-handled spoon, clean the inside of the pumpkin, being careful not to puncture the sides or the bottom.

When the pumpkin is clean, rinse the inside with cool water, checking for leaks in the skin. Fill the pumpkin with the hot punch and replace the lid to retain the heat. Ladle the warm punch into mugs and garnish with a cinnamon stick.

◀ Sangria ▶

Sangria, one of the world's oldest and most noble punches, is a blend of wine, brandy, fresh fruit, and soda water (though it has innumerable variations). Try a good Spanish Rioja to make a traditional red sangria; use white wine to make sangria blanco (white sangria); or get a bottle of Spanish cava to make sparkling sangria. As with a good stew, the better the ingredients, the better the taste.

SERVES 14 TO 16

Two 750 ml bottles Spanish Rioja, Beaujolais Nouveau, or
other light dry red wine

4 ounces Cognac

4 ounces Grand Marnier

$1/2$ cup sugar

2 large apples, cored, peeled, and sliced

3 peaches, pitted and sliced

2 liters club soda, chilled

Combine all ingredients except the club soda and transfer to covered containers. Refrigerate overnight. When ready to serve, pour fruit mixture into 2 quart-sized pitchers and top off each with a liter of club soda. Stir gently with a wooden spoon, and serve with spoons in the pitchers. Guests can use the spoon to hold back the solids when filling their glasses, or to scoop out a slice or two of fruit.

Christmas Champagne Punch

PHOTOGRAPH ON PAGE 58

A good Champagne punch is always light and refreshing, and appropriate for any party—afternoon or evening. It's simple to make, and looks beautiful out on the bar or sideboard. It's important to use a decent brut Champagne; many moderately priced Champagnes and sparkling wines fit this category. This punch uses a flavorful ice ring to keep it at the perfect temperature throughout the evening.

SERVES 12 TO 15

For the Punch:
Two 750 ml bottles brut Champagne or
other dry sparkling wine, chilled
2 liters ginger ale, chilled
16 ounces lemonade (page 24), chilled
16 ounces orange juice, no pulp, chilled
15 strawberries, sliced
15 whole strawberries

For the Ice Ring:
Lemonade (page 24)
Sliced strawberries

MAKE THE PUNCH:

In a large (6-quart minimum) punch bowl, combine the Champagne, ginger ale, lemonade, and orange juice. Depending on taste, you can strengthen the punch by adding an extra bottle of Champagne, or temper it by increasing the amount of orange juice. Add the sliced strawberries directly to the punch. Cut a slit in each whole strawberry and garnish the rim of the bowl with them.

MAKE THE ICE RING:

Find a gelatin mold of appropriate size for the punch bowl you plan to use; the ring should fit comfortably in the bowl, leaving plenty of room for the punch. Fill the ring with the lemonade and fresh strawberries, and place in the freezer until solid, approximately $1^{1}/_{2}$ hours.

Remove the ice ring from the mold by placing the mold, open side down, on a flat, even surface. Gently tap the top of the mold to loosen the ring, then wiggle the sides while pulling the mold upward until the ice releases. Don't put the ring into the bowl until you're ready to serve the punch. (See photographs on page 59.)

Making the ice ring (CLOCKWISE FROM TOP LEFT): Adding fruit to the mold; filling the mold with liquid of choice; after freezing, loosening the ice ring by immersing the mold in a bowl of warm water; unmolding the ice ring into the punch bowl. (*For complete instructions, see page 57*). OPPOSITE: **Christmas Champagne Punch** (*recipe page 56*).

◄ New Year's Eve Punch ►

Here's a variation on Champagne punch, dressed up for New Year's with a touch of Cognac for extra punch and some triple sec for flavor. You can serve this directly over ice, or with ice in a bucket on the side, or make an ice ring by freezing a small portion of the juices in a ring mold.

SERVES 25

1 cup freshly squeezed lemon juice
(from about 5 large lemons), strained
1 cup orange juice
1 cup pineapple juice
1 cup triple sec
⅔ cup grenadine
2 cups Cognac
Three 750 ml bottles Champagne or other dry sparkling wine
2 oranges, sliced into wheels, for garnish

In a large bowl, combine the juices, triple sec, grenadine, and Cognac. Transfer the mixture into containers and refrigerate until ready to serve. Prior to serving, chill your punch bowl with ice cubes. When the bowl is cold, remove the ice, and replace with a frozen ice ring or fresh ice cubes. Pour the punch mixture into the bowl, add the Champagne and orange wheels, and stir gently. Serve immediately.

Cold Spiced Rum and Tea Punch

The sweet/spicy flavor of spiced rum balances with the astringency of tea and the sweetness of fresh fruit juices to produce a deliciously tangy punch appropriate for any occasion. Keep it cool with a large block of ice, or combine a small amount of the nonalcoholic ingredients to form an ice ring (see page 57).

SERVES 12

1½ cups freshly brewed breakfast-type tea

½ cup sugar

1½ cups spiced rum

2 ounces Grand Marnier

2 ounces triple sec

1 ounce grenadine

2 cups freshly squeezed orange juice

2 cups cranberry juice cocktail

12 lemon twists (see page 15)

In a saucepan, stir the brewed tea and sugar together over medium heat until the sugar is dissolved, about 2 minutes. Pour into a medium bowl and place in the refrigerator to cool. In a punch bowl, combine the rum, Grand Marnier, triple sec, grenadine, and fruit juices. Stir in the sweetened tea. Serve over ice in tall highball glasses, garnished with the lemon twists.

Sherbet Punch

Unless you live in a biker bar, you are bound to have some nondrinkers at your next party. Whether it's for children, teetotalers, or designated drivers, as a gracious host you ought to make the party special for everyone. The nondrinker usually gets handed a Pellegrino with lime and is forgotten about, while the rest of the crew drinks all manner of fabulous cocktails. Instead, why not make a tart nonalcoholic punch that everyone can enjoy?

SERVES 20 TO 24

24 ounces lemonade (page 24)
16 strawberries
2 quarts lime sherbet, softened at room temperature for 30 minutes
4 liters carbonated Tom Collins mix

First, make an ice ring. Combine the lemonade and strawberries in a gelatin mold. Cover with plastic wrap and freeze until solid.

When the ice ring is ready, combine the softened sherbet with all but 1 cup of the Tom Collins mix, and beat with a whisk. Add the reserved cup of mix just prior to serving, to give the punch extra carbonation. Serve in a large punch bowl with the fruited ice ring.

Cranberry Tea Punch

Cranberries have been part of the American holiday tradition since the first Thanksgiving in 1621. High in vitamin C, cranberries spring from small evergreen shrubs that grow in mountainous forests and bogs from Alaska down to Tennessee. Because cranberries are one of only three fruits indigenous to North America (the Concord grape and the blueberry are the other two), they are a unique part of the American holiday tradition. The tart flavor of cranberry juice combined with tea, sweet brown sugar, and spices makes for a holiday punch that's wonderful served warm or chilled over ice.

SERVES 10 TO 12

6 bags Earl Grey tea (or other breakfast-type blend)
1 cup packed brown sugar
½ teaspoon ground cloves
2 cinnamon sticks
16 ounces unsweetened cranberry juice
16 ounces apple cider
1 large lemon, sliced thinly into wheels

In a large pot, bring 1 quart of water to a boil and add the 6 tea bags. Remove from the heat. Steep for about 10 minutes to get a fairly strong tea, then remove the teabags.

Return the pot to high heat and add the sugar, cloves, and cinnamon sticks. Stir frequently until all the sugar is dissolved, about 2 minutes. Remove from the heat and add the cranberry juice and apple cider. Float lemon wheels on top as a garnish.

MAKING FRESH CRANBERRY JUICE FOR PUNCHES

PREPARING FRESH cranberry juice at home is simple. Purchase a 12-ounce package of fresh cranberries, and wash them thoroughly, sorting out mushy or rotten berries as you rinse them. Place the berries in a large saucepan, and pour in water until the berries are just covered. Bring the mixture to a rapid boil on high heat, then reduce heat to a simmer and cover. Simmer for 10 minutes, or until the cranberries pop and become soft. Strain the berries through a fine-mesh sieve into a large bowl and add enough water to make 2 quarts of juice. This juice may be refrigerated for up to a week. To sweeten the juice (you don't have to, by the way) add ²/₃ cup of honey. Makes 2 quarts.

4

CLASSIC HOLIDAY COCKTAILS

Poinsettia

PHOTOGRAPH ON PAGE 66

Two of the most popular holiday staples, cranberries and Champagne, join forces in this holiday classic blazing with festive color. It's a drink of fairly recent origin, with quite a few variations: I've seen it made with triple sec, Cointreau, and Grand Marnier. I prefer a small splash of Cointreau, the clear orange liqueur made from both sweet and bitter orange peels.

SERVES 8

1 large orange

8 ounces Cointreau, triple sec, or
Grand Marnier, chilled

16 ounces cranberry juice cocktail, chilled

Two 750 ml bottles Champagne, or other
dry sparkling wine, chilled

Using a vegetable peeler or a small paring knife, remove the zest from the orange in long, $1/2$-inch-wide strips, avoiding the bitter, white pith. Pour 1 ounce of Cointreau and 2 ounces of cranberry juice into the bottom of each martini glass (or use large Champagne glasses). Fill the glass with Champagne, and garnish with an orange twist.

Kir Royale

It is said that monks first produced crème de cassis in the sixteenth century as a cure for snakebites and overall "wretchedness." Whether this is true or not, this black currant liqueur is certainly the cure for a wretched bottle of Champagne. But don't limit yourself to an average cocktail; Kir Royale is even better if you use a decent—even very good—bottle of Champagne. You might also want to try substituting the cassis with a splash of Chambord, the delicious French black raspberry liqueur, to make a variation known as (what else?) a Chambord.

SERVES 8

8 ounces crème de cassis
Two 750 ml bottles Champagne, well chilled
8 lemon twists (see page 15)

Pour 1 ounce of crème de cassis into the bottom of a flute—the taller the better. Top off with well-chilled Champagne, and garnish with a lemon twist.

Chocolate Martini

While I haven't given up on the old gin martini completely, I order this recent martini innovation whenever I have the chance. If you love a strong drink and you enjoy the flavor of chocolate, look no further. But a word of caution: these are just as strong as regular martinis, so don't let the taste fool you.

SERVES 10

¼ cup unsweetened cocoa powder
10 Hershey's Kisses (or 4 ounces finely grated chocolate)
20 ounces vodka (preferably vanilla-infused)
10 ounces white crème de cacao

Prepare 10 martini glasses by moistening their rims with water and placing them in the freezer for about 20 minutes. When the glasses are chilled, spread the cocoa powder in a thin layer on a plate, and "salt" the rims by pressing them into the cocoa. Place a Hershey's Kiss or half an ounce of grated chocolate at the bottom of each glass.

In a cocktail shaker, combine the vodka and crème de cacao with plenty of ice. Shake until mixture is well chilled, and strain into the prepared martini glasses.

Champagne Cocktail

Every year, I end up with several bottles of mediocre sparkling wine stockpiled in the back of my refrigerator, usually gifts from guests or leftovers from one party or another. Not good enough to "regift," but not bad enough to throw away, these bottles seem to occupy a vinous netherworld, patiently waiting their turn to be uncorked. If you have such a bottle or two, here's an elegant solution: the Champagne cocktail. It's unbeliev-able what a sugar cube, a dash of bitters, and twist of lemon will do to an unremarkable bottle of sparkling wine. And Champagne cocktails are the perfect way to kick off any-thing from a small dinner party to a huge Christmas Eve gathering.

SERVES 12

12 sugar cubes
(or 12 dashes simple syrup; see page 24)
36 dashes angostura bitters
72 ounces Champagne or other sparkling white wine, chilled
12 lemon twists (see page 15)

Soak each sugar cube with 3 dashes of bitters, and place one in the bottom of each flute. Pour Champagne to the top, and garnish with a lemon twist.

Mimosa

The mimosa has long been a delicious staple of Sunday brunch and, along with the Bloody Mary, even a hangover helper. A simple mix of orange juice and sparkling wine (Champagne if you're lucky), the mimosa can turn a late breakfast of eggs and bacon into a noontime party—while soothing the effects of that imprudent 1:00 A.M. flute of bubbly. Augment the mimosa with some triple sec, the orange liqueur, and you have a morning glory, a slightly more potent and festive cocktail.

SERVES 12

24 ounces orange juice
Two 750 ml bottles sparkling white wine or Champagne
12 orange wheels or twists (see page 15)

Pour 2 ounces of orange juice into each of 12 tall flutes. Fill to the top with sparkling wine or Champagne, and garnish with an orange wheel or twist.

Candy Cane

Layered drinks such as the pousse-café, a cocktail featuring five separate liquors of varying density—each layer balancing gently on the other—are a unique testament to a bartender's skill and an unusual drinking experience. Layered cocktails are meant to be sipped one layer at a time, giving the drinker a variety of tastes—and perhaps a healthy buzz, depending on the number of layers. To create the Candy Cane, a holiday-themed shot, alternate white peppermint liqueur and red, almond-flavored crème de noyeaux in a tall shot glass. This drink will get your next holiday party off to a raging start.

SERVES 12

12 ounces Rumple Minze
(or other white, peppermint-flavored liqueur)
6 ounces red crème de noyeaux

Chill the liqueurs thoroughly in the freezer. Pour a quarter-inch layer of peppermint liqueur into each shot glass (tall, thin ones if you can find them). Carefully spoon a quarter inch layer of crème de noyeaux on top. Repeat twice, until you have a shot glass that resembles a liquid candy cane. Serve immediately, while still cold.

Christmas Champagne Cheer

This variation on the mimosa uses frozen cranberry juice, Champagne, and a splash of lime juice to create the perfect Christmas morning cocktail. Using frozen juice concentrate is a wonderful way to create chilled Champagne drinks infused with intense fruit flavor. This variation uses frozen cranberry juice, but if you use orange juice concentrate you'll end up with a wonderful mimosa cheer.

SERVES 8

**8 ounces frozen cranberry juice concentrate,
thawed at room temperature for 30 minutes
2 limes, 1 juiced and the other cut into 8 wedges
One 750 ml bottle Champagne or
other dry sparkling white wine**

Place the frozen juice mix in a large pitcher and use a long-handled spoon to break up any chunks. Add lime juice, top with the Champagne, and stir gently. Serve in tall flutes or white-wine glasses, garnished with lime wedges.

Café Torino Riviera Cocktail

Turin boasts some astounding Baroque architecture, but more important, it is home to the famous Riviera cocktail, ladled from a punch bowl directly into your glass. My good friend and longtime Bologna resident Andrea Pandolfini sent me this recipe and explained: "The Torino uses prosecco in the punch, but I've made it in the States with other sparkling wines. Just make sure not to overdo it with the Campari."

SERVES 16

4 ounces Mandarine Napoléon
4 ounces vodka
16 ounces grapefruit juice
4 ounces Campari
12 ounces prosecco or other dry sparkling white wine
1 orange, sliced into wheels
1 peach, sliced into wedges
1-pound can pineapple slices in unsweetened juice, drained
1 cup strawberries, for garnish
Small skewers

Combine all of the ingredients except the strawberries in a punch bowl. Stir vigorously. Ladle into glasses and serve garnished with a skewered strawberry.

Bloody Mary

Ever since a Frenchman named Pete Petiot mixed the first Bloody Mary at Harry's New York Bar in Paris in the 1920s, it's been the world's favorite morning and afternoon cocktail. The ingredients of the Bloody are almost as unusual as its birth: an unlikely convergence of canned tomato juice, vodka, and Worcestershire. M. Petiot had been concocting a morning drink, known as the tomato cocktail, previous to his invention, but found newly arrived vodka (brought by Russian expatriates) to provide the perfect "pick-up" for wounded tipplers. It's also the perfect drink for a holiday brunch.

SERVES 12

24 ounces vodka

48 ounces tomato juice

½ cup freshly squeezed lemon juice (from 2 to 3 lemons)

3 ounces Worcestershire sauce

2 teaspoons cayenne pepper

6 teaspoons prepared horseradish

2 teaspoons celery salt

2 limes, cut into 12 wedges

Fill a large pitcher (or two smaller ones) with the vodka, tomato juice, lemon juice, Worcestershire sauce, cayenne pepper, horseradish, and celery salt. Stir thoroughly. Pour into ice-filled glasses, garnishing each with a wedge of lime.

Bloody Caesar

If there's anything better than a tall Bloody Mary on Christmas or New Year's morning, it's a Bloody Caesar. Once you experience a properly prepared Bloody Caesar, you may never want a plain Bloody Mary again. You can make this drink two ways. If you can find a bottled clam juice that isn't too salty (I have yet to find one), simply add about an ounce of it to each regular Bloody Mary. The more reliable method is to use Clamato-brand tomato cocktail, whose flavor is perfectly balanced between salty and tangy. Replace the vodka with more Clamato juice to make virgin Bloody Caesars.

SERVES 12

12 ounces vodka

24 ounces Clamato juice

2 teaspoons prepared horseradish

12 dashes hot sauce, such as Tabasco

4 teaspoons Worcestershire sauce

Salt and pepper to taste

12 skewers of freshly shucked clams
(see opposite)

2 celery stalks, trimmed and cut into
3-inch segments

Combine vodka, Clamato, horseradish, hot sauce, Worcestershire sauce, salt, and pepper in a mixing glass and stir well. Pour into ice-filled glasses, and garnish with a skewered freshly shucked clam and a celery stick. Or substitute a boiled, peeled shrimp for the clam skewer.

Shucked Clam Skewers

12 littleneck clams (or substitute oysters)
12 medium-sized wooden skewers

Using a thick, folded dish towel, hold the clam in one hand and a shucking knife (not a regular kitchen knife) in the other. Insert the blade near the hinge and twist to spread the shells slightly apart. Run the knife around the rest of the shell, making sure that most of the circumference is free. Lifting the top shell, reach in with the knife to cut through the hinge muscle. Remove the clam and slide it onto the skewer.

COFFEES, COCOAS, AND TEAS

Irish Coffee

PHOTOGRAPH ON PAGE 86

Although I'm sure that many a dash of whiskey has made it into a coffee mug over the centuries, it wasn't until the 1940s that Irish coffee was officially invented. The most interesting story of the drink's origin claims it dates back to Ireland's Shannon Airport in the early years of transatlantic air travel. It seems the drink was concocted by one Joe Sheridan to soothe shaken passengers who'd flown through hard storms in their "flying boats." Sipping the smooth elixir, one passenger supposedly asked if he was drinking Brazilian coffee. To which Mr. Sheridan indignantly replied, "No, that's Irish coffee!"

SERVES 6

6 ounces Irish whiskey
30 ounces freshly brewed coffee
¼ cup sugar
1 cup heavy cream, chilled
1 tablespoon confectioners' sugar

Combine 1 ounce whiskey, 5 ounces coffee, and 2 teaspoons sugar in a mug (ideally a clear glass one). In a medium bowl, whip the cream with the confectioners' sugar until it's slightly thickened. Using the back of a spoon, carefully slip the whipped cream into the mug, so that it rests on top of the coffee without dissolving into it.

Hot Chocolate

PHOTOGRAPH ON PAGE 87

Considering how simple it is to make real hot chocolate, it's a shame how few people ever make it. No matter how much you love instant hot chocolate mixes, there is just no comparison with the depth of chocolate flavor in homemade hot chocolate.

SERVES 10 TO 12

½ cup heavy cream
6 cups whole milk
3 teaspoons vanilla extract
¼ teaspoon salt
1 pint heavy cream, chilled, for whipping
2 tablespoons confectioners' sugar
12 ounces bittersweet chocolate, finely chopped
Grated bittersweet chocolate, for garnish

In a saucepan over medium heat, mix the ½ cup cream, milk, vanilla, and salt, and slowly bring to a boil. Whip the pint of cream with the confectioners' sugar until soft peaks form; set aside. Place chopped chocolate into a small pot or heavy bowl. Melt by pouring the hot milk mixture on top, and thoroughly whisking until all the chocolate is melted. Pour the melted chocolate back into the saucepan. Stir well, heat until steaming, and remove from heat. Serve immediately with fresh whipped cream and chocolate shavings on top.

ABOVE: **Hot Chocolate** *(recipe page 85)*. OPPOSITE: **Irish Coffee** *(recipe page 84)*.

Candy Cane Cocoa

This recipe livens up rich hot chocolate, adding a touch of holiday cheer with crème de menthe, the mint liqueur, and some delicious peppermint whipped cream made with candy canes.

SERVES 4

For the Hot Cocoa:
¾ cup unsweetened cocoa powder
½ cup sugar
1½ teaspoons vanilla extract
Pinch salt
3½ cups whole milk
½ cup heavy cream
4 ounces crème de menthe

For the Peppermint Whipped Cream:
4 candy canes
1 cup heavy cream, chilled

4 candy canes, for garnish

MAKE THE COCOA:

In a heavy saucepan, combine $^1/_2$ cup of water with the cocoa powder, sugar, vanilla, and salt over low heat. Whisking frequently, cook until the mixture is smooth. In a separate pot, combine the milk and cream and heat until just boiling. Gradually whisk the hot milk into the chocolate paste until completely blended; keep warm.

MAKE THE PEPPERMINT WHIPPED CREAM:

Place four candy canes into a doubled plastic bag and pound with a rolling pin until finely pulverized. In a medium bowl, whip the cream to soft peaks, then fold in the peppermint pieces.

To serve, pour an ounce of crème de menthe into a mug and top off with hot cocoa. Stir, then garnish with the peppermint whipped cream and a candy cane stirrer.

Vanilla Nutmeg Coffee

I can honestly remember a time when there was no such thing as flavored coffee—or, at least, it seemed like it. Except for holidays and special occasions, coffee was simply coffee: a twenty-five cent cup of Joe, served in a paper cup that (if you lived in New York) invariably said, "It's Our Pleasure to Serve You." Times have sure changed. Now, there are about a hundred different ways to have your morning coffee, Starbucks is more expensive than gas on a gallon-to-gallon basis, and flavored coffees are routine. This recipe harkens back to gentler times when flavored coffees were something you sipped after a holiday meal in front of a roaring hearth.

SERVES 8

1 vanilla bean, coarsely chopped
½ cup coffee beans
¾ teaspoon ground nutmeg
2 cinnamon sticks

Note: You'll need a coffee grinder to extract the maximum flavor from the coffee and vanilla beans. However, if you don't have a coffee grinder, place ⅓ cup of preground coffee in the filter basket, along with one finely chopped vanilla bean, and proceed as usual.

Place the chopped vanilla bean and coffee beans in a coffee grinder and grind. Fill the filter basket halfway with coffee, add the ground nutmeg, and pour in the rest

of the coffee. Place the cinnamon sticks in the coffee pot, and brew using 6 cups of water. After brewing, let stand (on the heating plate) for at least five minutes. Remove the cinnamon sticks and serve.

COFFEES, COCOAS, AND TEAS

Mexican Coffee

I don't think there's a plaque celebrating Mexican coffee anywhere—or any dispute over its origin, for that matter. There are, however, many fans of this Irish coffee variation, which uses coffee-flavored liqueur instead of Irish whiskey, making for a sweeter—and very delicious—drink. Mexican Kahlúa is the traditional brand of choice, although nowadays there are many other excellent coffee liqueurs to choose from.

SERVES 6

6 ounces Kahlúa
(or other coffee-flavored liqueur)
30 ounces freshly brewed coffee
¼ cup sugar
1 cup heavy cream, chilled
1 tablespoon confectioners' sugar

Combine 1 ounce Kahlúa, 5 ounces hot coffee, and 2 teaspoons sugar in a mug. In a medium bowl, whip the cream with the confectioners' sugar until it's slightly thickened. Using the back of a spoon, carefully slip the whipped cream into the mug, so that it rests on top of the coffee without dissolving into it.

Witches' Yule Tea

Modern-day witches, known as Wiccans, celebrate a winter solstice festival called Yule right around December 21st. According to their Book of Shadows, this is the appropriate tea to drink while celebrating an authentic Yule. I think it's delicious year-round.

SERVES 8

Peel from half a lemon
5 whole cloves
4 cinnamon sticks
1 teaspoon allspice berries
1 whole nutmeg
1 bay leaf
1 teaspoon dried chamomile
8 teabags of black tea
1 apple, peeled and thinly sliced

Stud the lemon peel with the cloves, and place in a square of cheesecloth along with the remaining spices and chamomile. Tie the sachet using kitchen string and place in a large pot or tea pot along with the teabags. Bring 6 cups of water to a rolling boil in a separate pot and pour over the sachet and teabags. Allow to steep for at least three minutes, then serve the tea in mugs with the apple slices floating on top.

Orange Spiced Tea

Whatever happened to "tea time"? It has become a thing of the past, relegated to old ladies and the hopelessly British, who seem to have plenty of time on their hands. But amidst the bustle of the holiday season, moments of respose are especially important. Enjoy them with this exquisite spiced tea.

SERVES 4

1 orange
5 whole cloves
Peel of half a lemon
2 cinnamon sticks
4 teabags of black tea
4 teaspoons sugar

Slice an orange in half and stud one half with the cloves, reserving the other half for another use. Place the studded orange half in a square of cheesecloth along with the lemon peel and cinnamon sticks and tie with kitchen string. Place the tea bags and spice sachet into a teapot. In a separate pot, bring 3 cups of water to a boil, pour into teapot, and allow to steep for 3 minutes, or until it reaches the desired strength. Remove tea bags and sachet, and pour the tea into mugs, with one teaspoon of sugar stirred into each.